NATIONAL GEOGRAPHIC

D0100649

Who Lives at the Zoo?

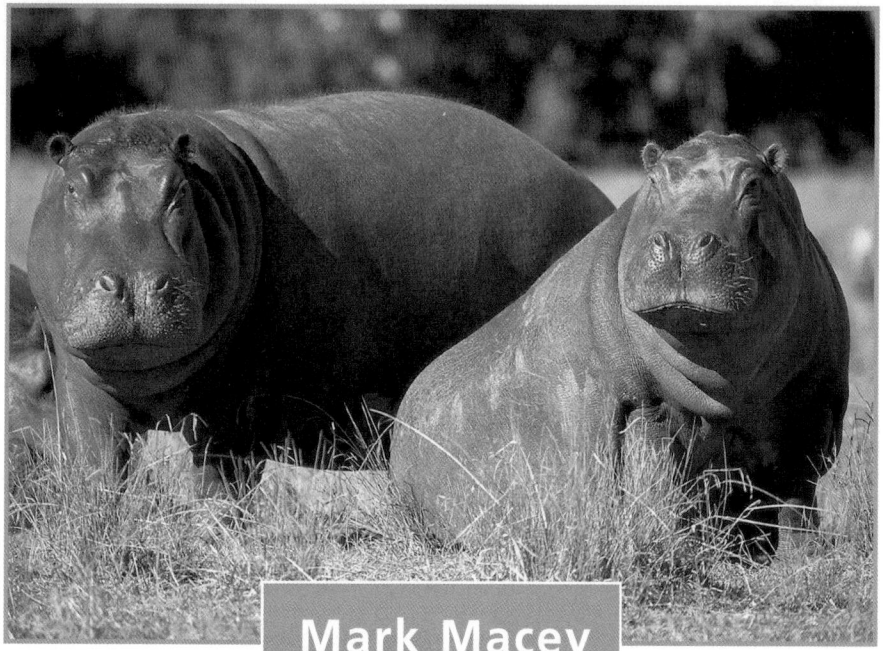

Mark Macey

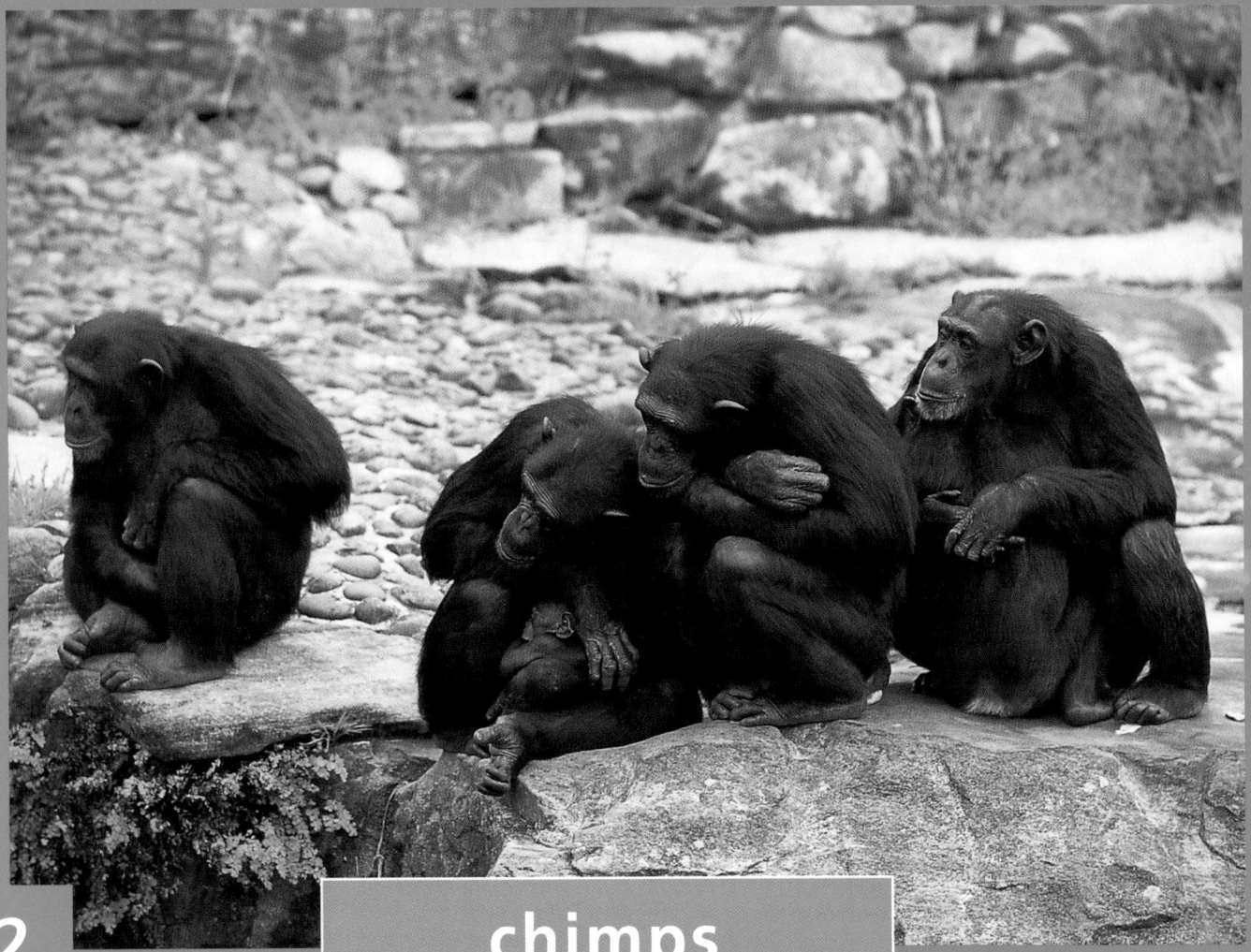

2 chimps

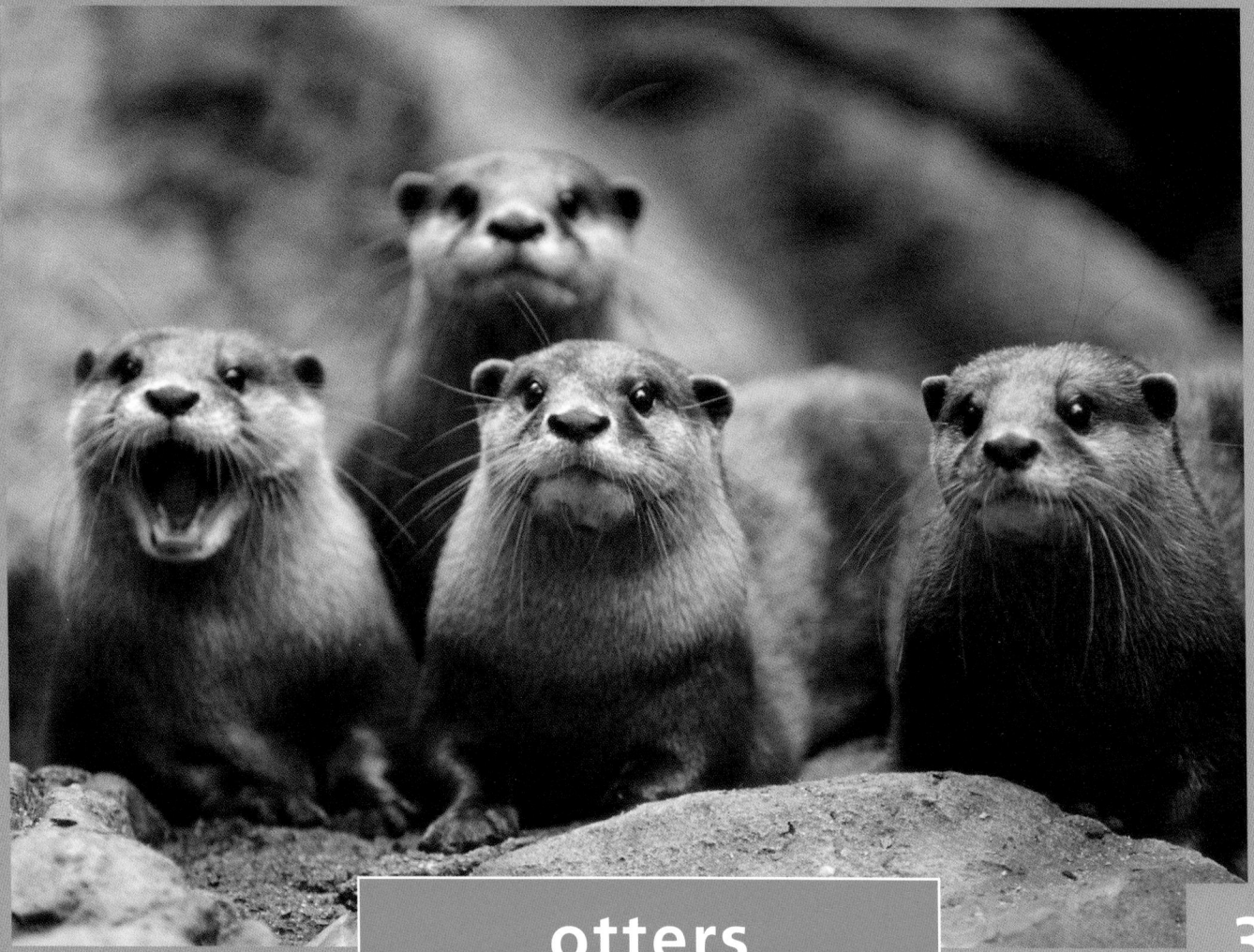

otters

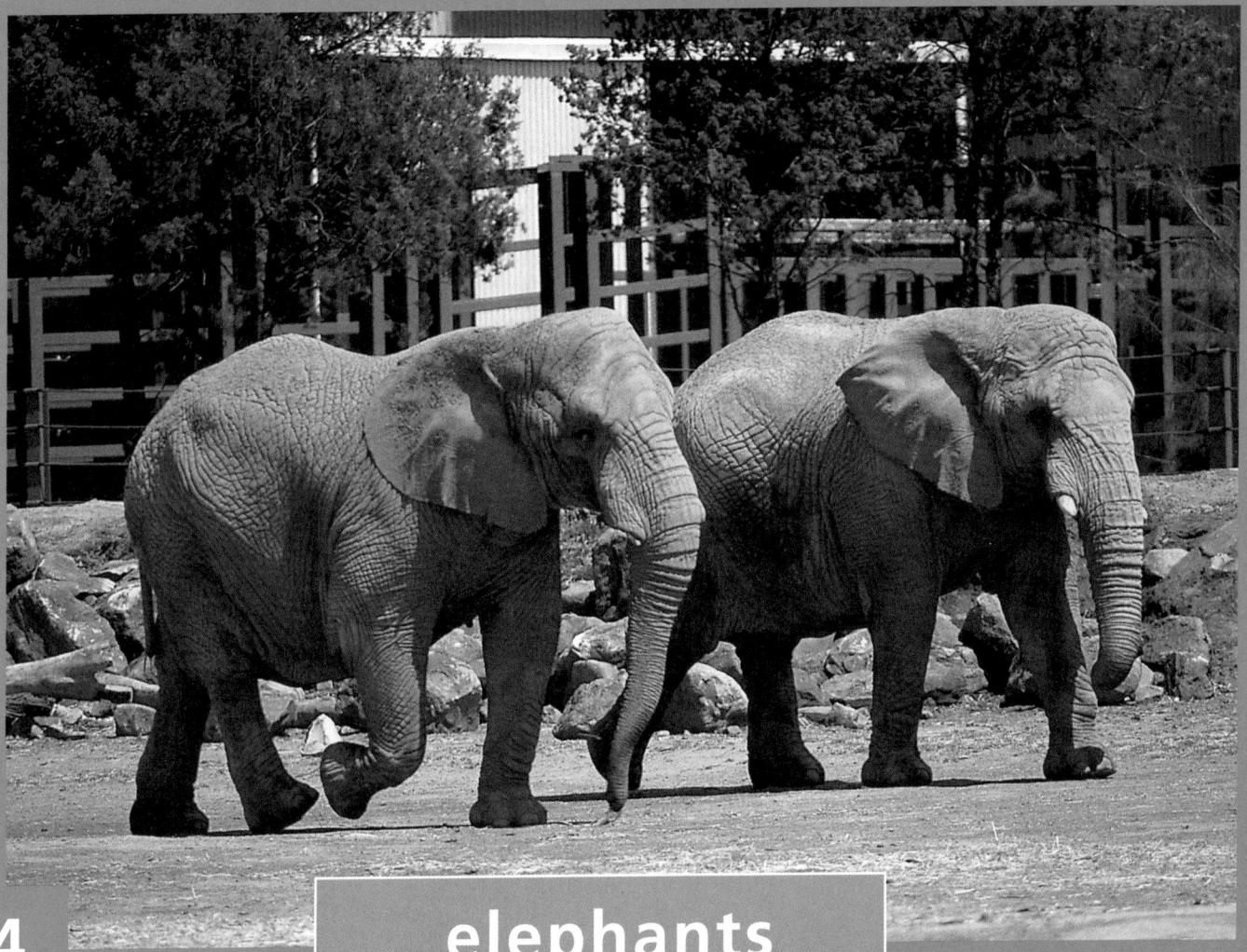

4 elephants

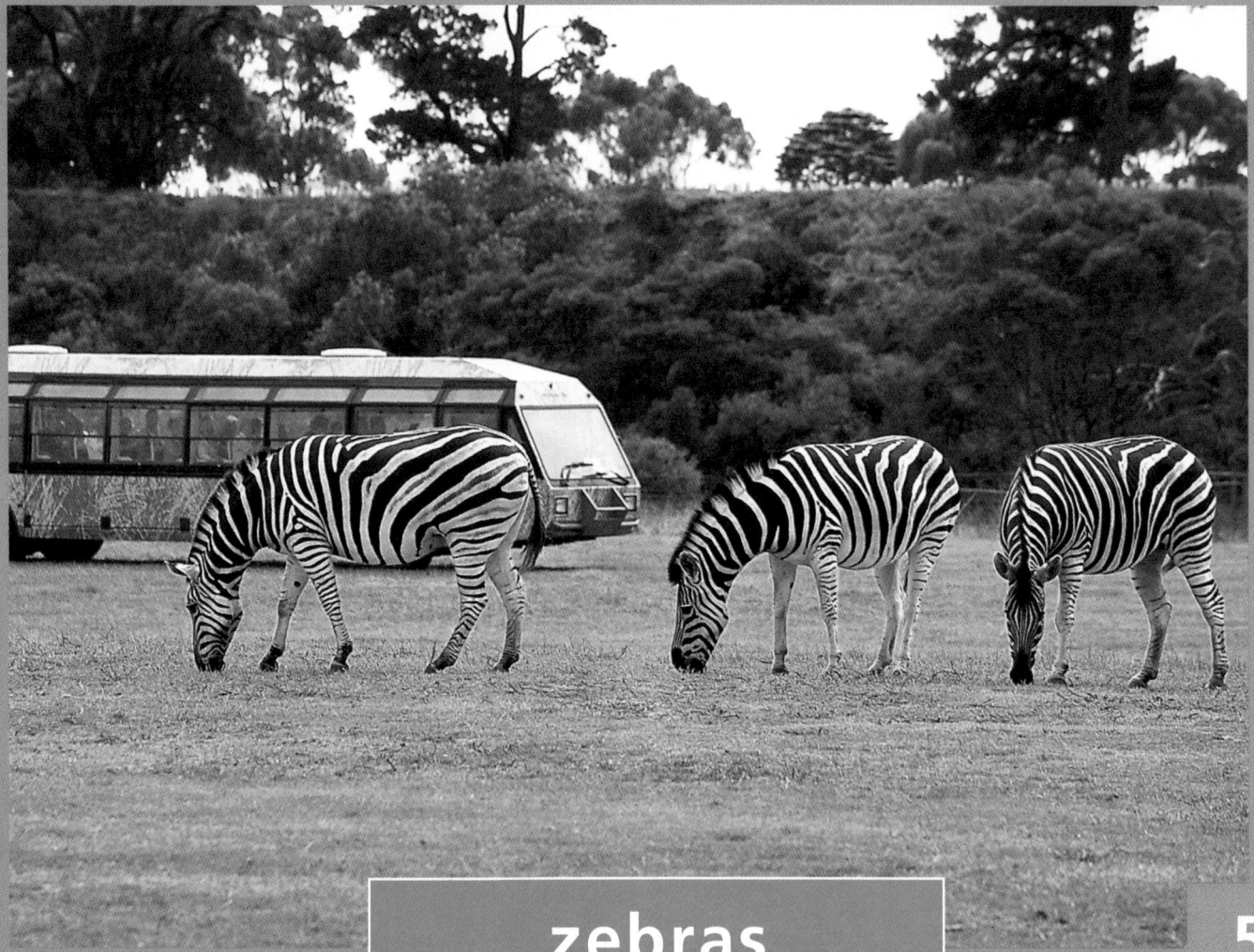

zebras

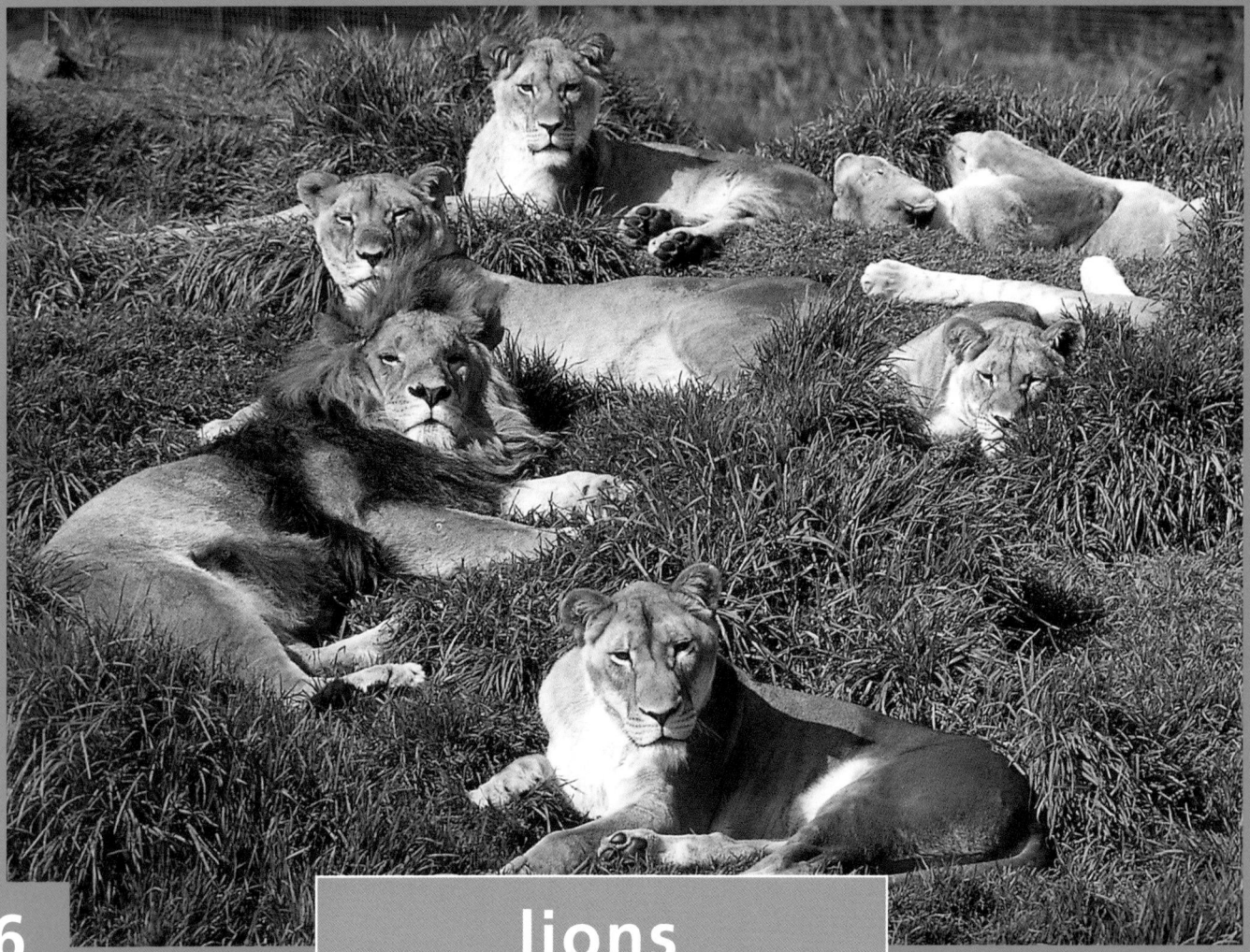

6

lions

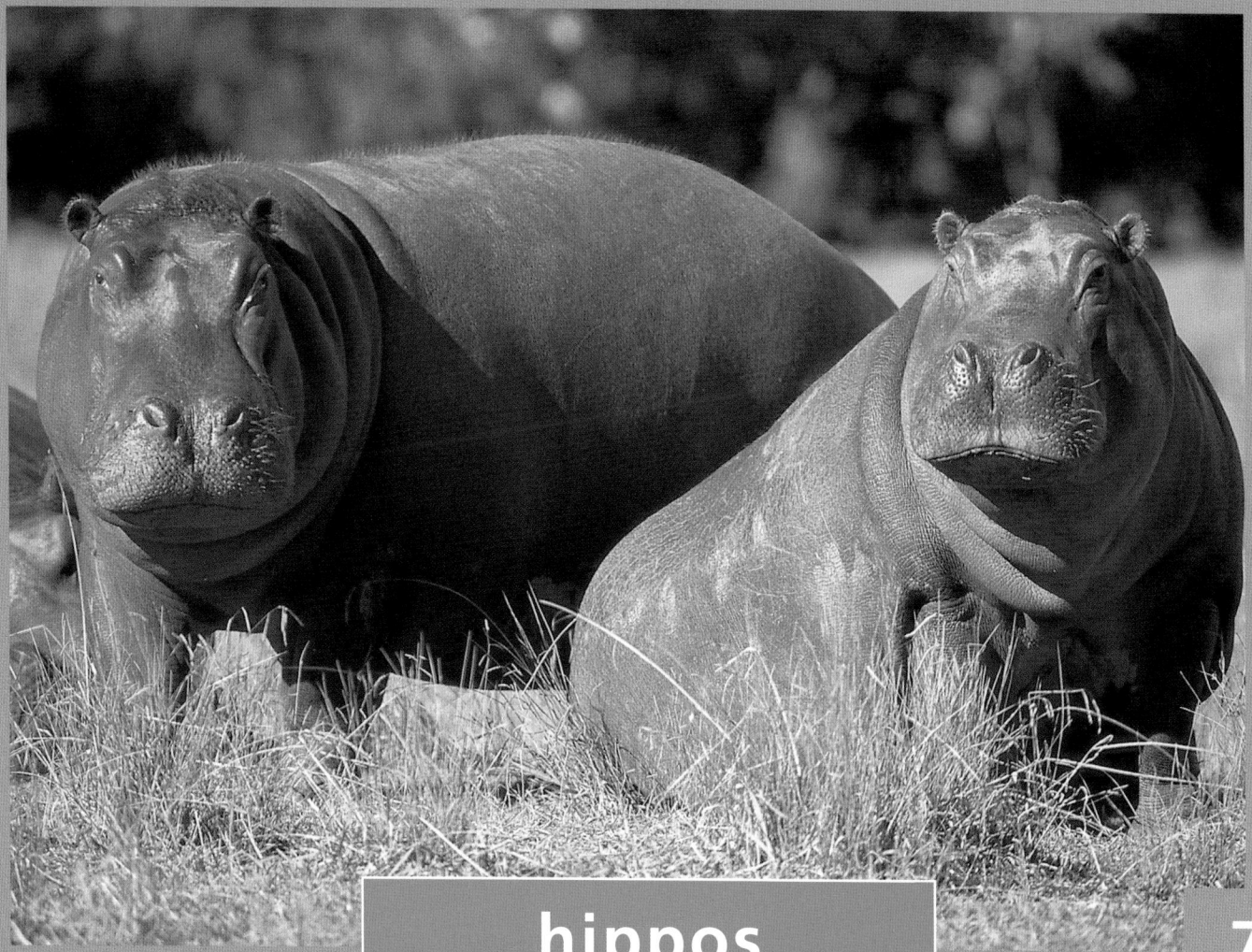

hippos

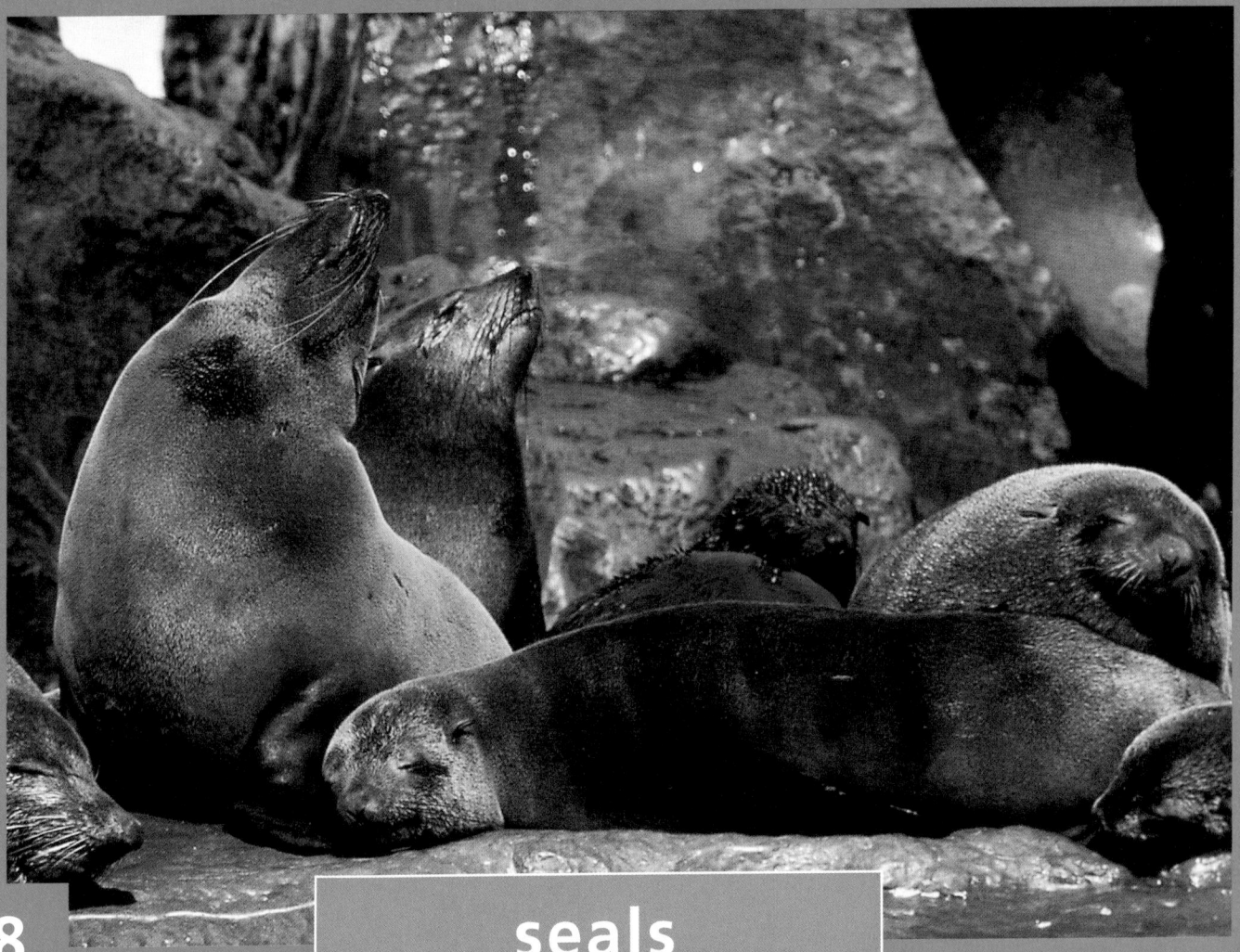

seals

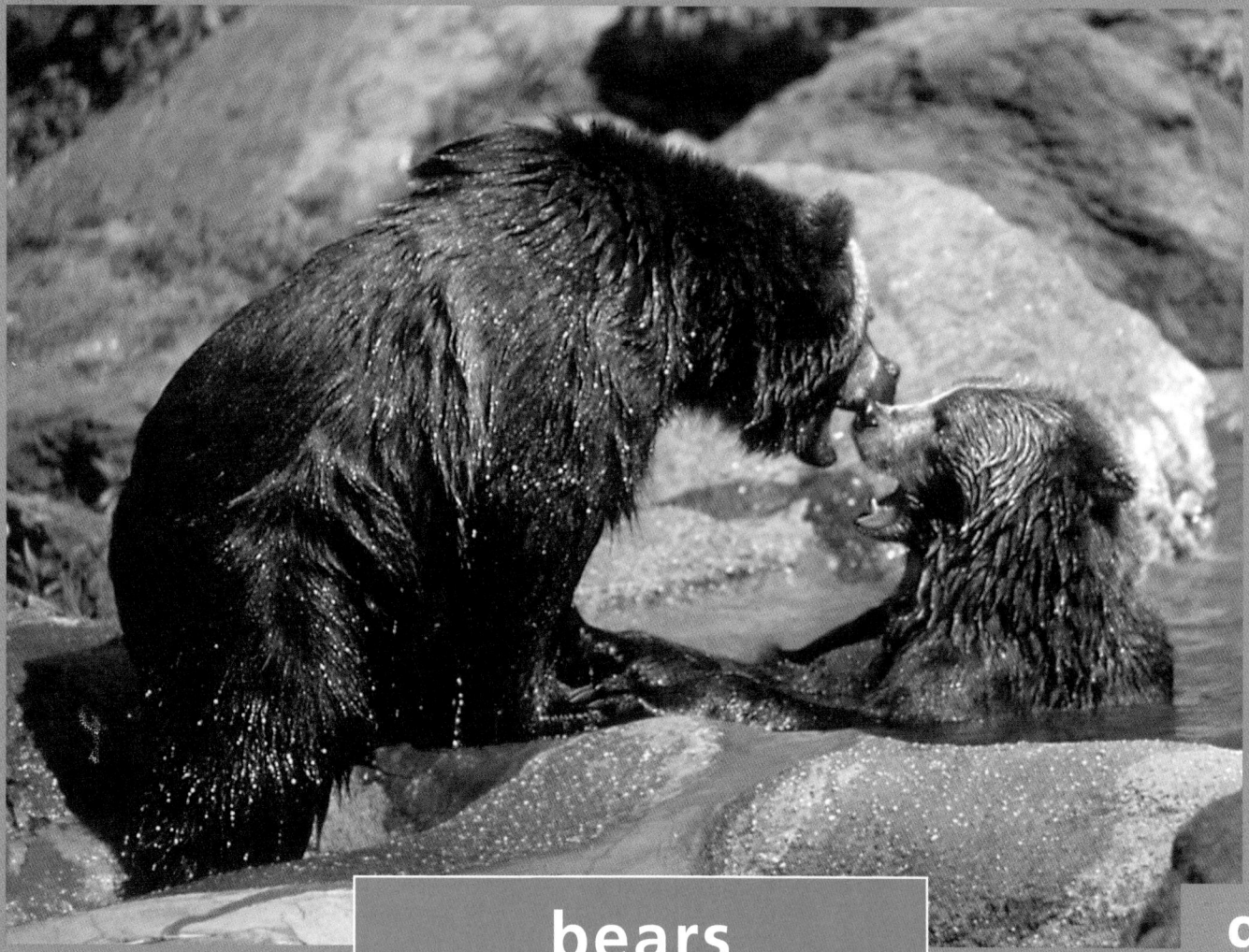

bears

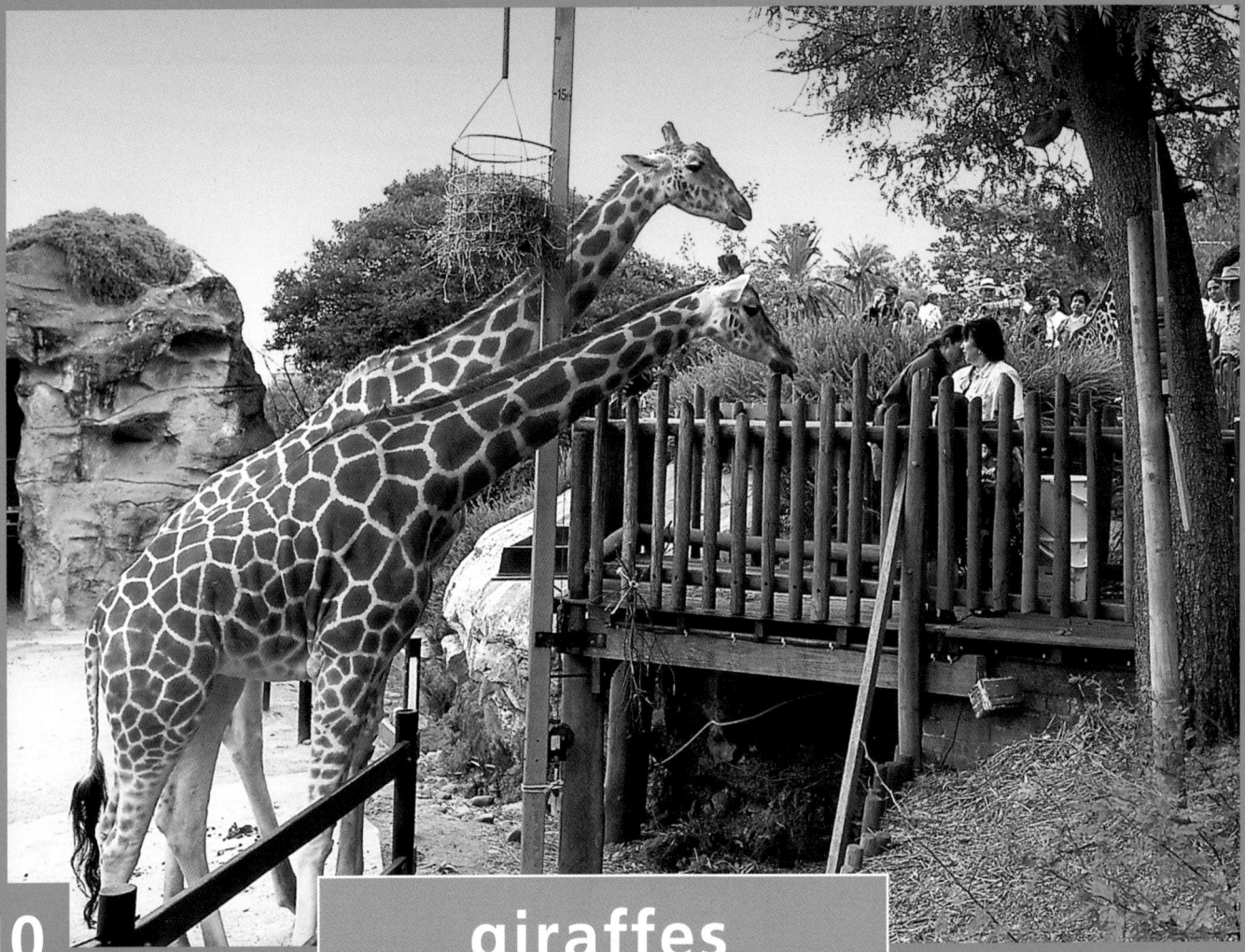

10

giraffes

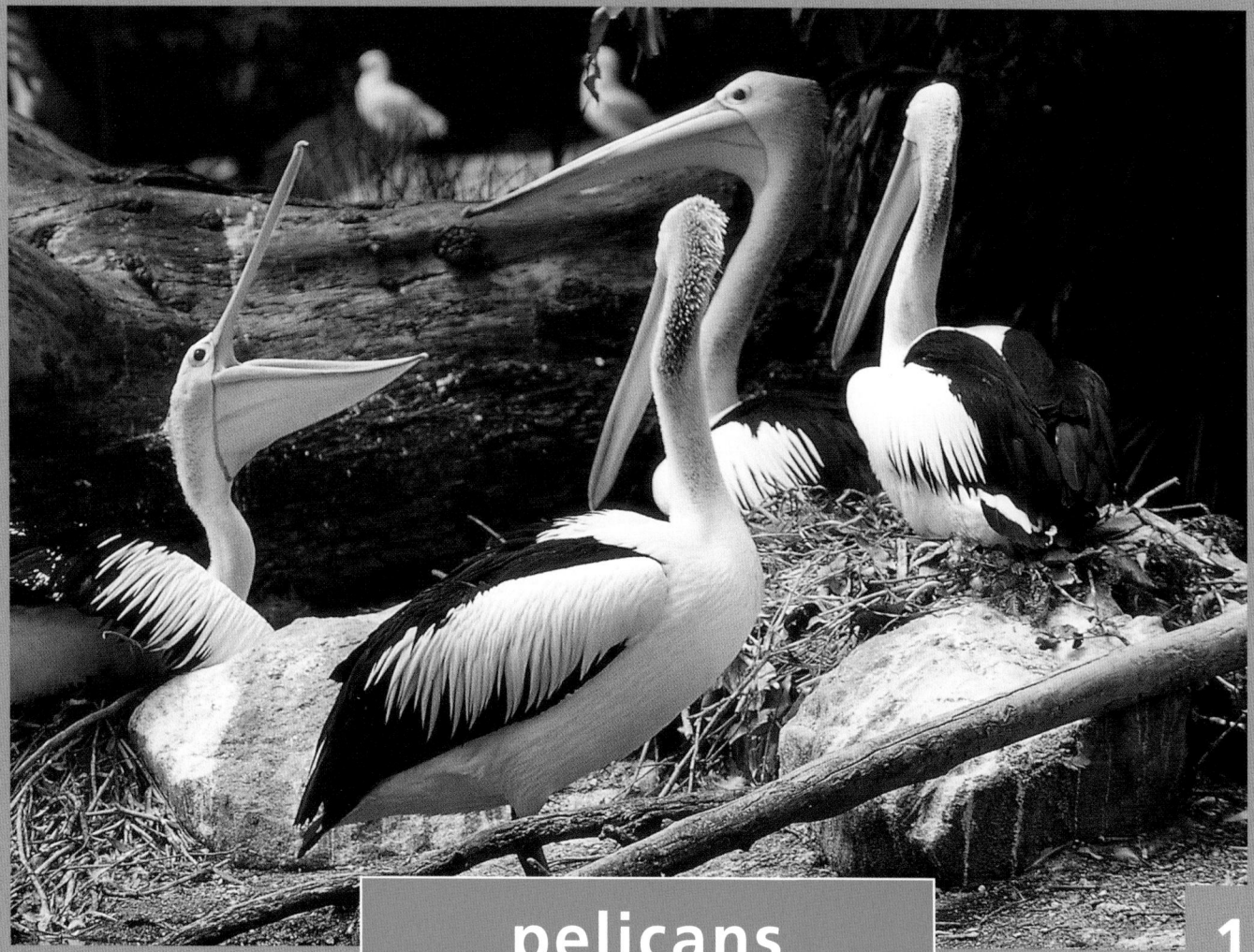

pelicans

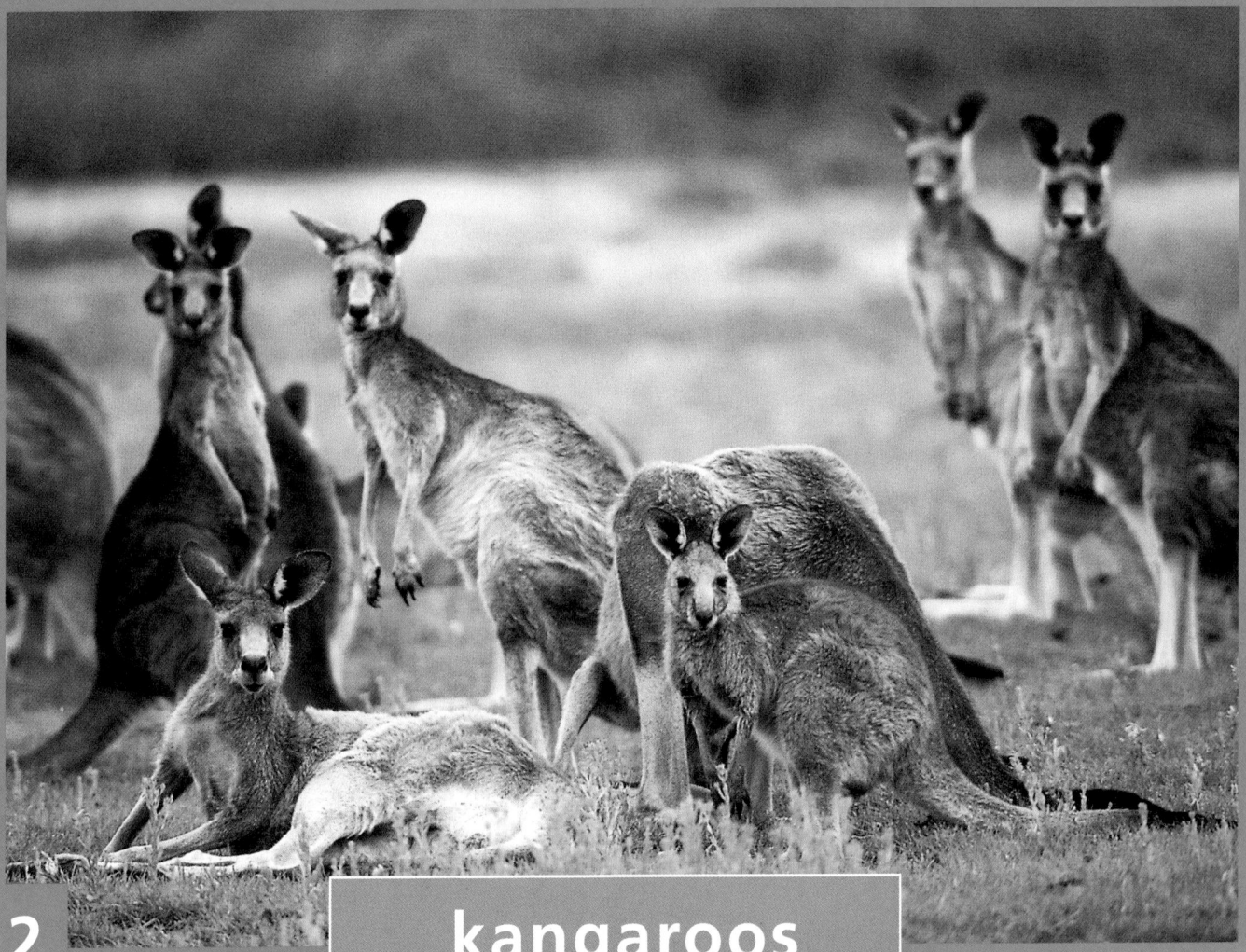

kangaroos